Cities

Jen Green

WAYLAND

First published in 2009 by Wayland

Copyright © Wayland 2009

Wayland
338 Euston Road
London NW1 3BH

Wayland Australia
Level 17/207 Kent Street
Sydney, NSW 2000

Senior editor: Camilla Lloyd
Designer: Simon Borrough
Consultant: Rob Bowden
Picture researcher: Shelley Noronha
Artwork: Ian Thompson
Sherlock Bones artwork: Richard Hook

Picture Acknowledgments: The author and publisher would like to thank the following for allowing their pictures to be reproduced in this publication:
Cover: © Michael Yamashita/Corbis; 1, 4, 6, 19, 22, 23, 24, 28, 29 (t) Digital Vision/Getty Images, 7 © Yann Arthus-Bertrand/Corbis, 8 © Hulton-Deutsch Collection/Corbis, 9 © Dinodia Images/Alamy, 10 © World Pictures/Alamy, 12 © Paulo Fridman/Corbis, 13, 16 © EASI-Images/Rob Bowden, 14 © Michael Yamashita/Corbis, 15 © Visions of America, LLC/Alamy, 17 © Christophe Boisvieux/Corbis, 18 © MAPS.com/Corbis, 20 © Ryan Pyle/Corbis, 21 ©David J. Phillip/Pool/epa/Corbis, 26 © Xin Zhu/Istock, 27 © Michael Willis/Alamy, 29 (b) © EASI-Images/Rob Bowden.

British Library Cataloguing in Publication Data:
Green, Jen
    Cities. - (The geography detective investigates)
    1. Cities and towns - Juvenile literature
    I. Title

307.7'6

ISBN: 978 0 7502 5674 2

Printed in China

Wayland is a division of Hachette Children's Books, an Hachette UK company.

www.hachette.co.uk

Contents

Words that appear in **bold** can be
found in the glossary on page 30.

**The Geography Detective, Sherlock Bones, will help you learn all about
Cities. The answers to Sherlock's questions can be found on page 31.**

What is a city?

Cities are large **settlements** where thousands of people live and work. As well as being home to large numbers of people, cities are also centres of business, industry and government. They provide a focus for culture and religion too.

FOCUS ON

Varied cultures

Cities often contain people from many different **ethnic** backgrounds. **Immigrants** who have arrived from abroad, often looking for work, become established in a particular part of the city, forming a community with a distinct character. For example, many cities have a 'Chinatown' where shops and restaurants are run by Chinese people.

Towns and cities are **urban** areas, containing a greater concentration of people than **rural** areas – the countryside. There is no clear distinction between a town and a **city**, but many experts call any settlement with more than 50,000 people a city. All cities have their own government in the form of a council, and capital cities are home to national governments too.

People from many different backgrounds live in cities like Barcelona. This creates a rich culture, but can sometimes cause tensions between people from different groups.

From the 1800s, cities in Europe and North America grew quickly. During the 1900s, cities expanded in other parts of the world, and some are still growing rapidly. Cities now cover large areas that were once countryside, and have transformed landscapes all over the world. Over half the world's **population** now lives in urban areas.

Life is generally more hectic in the city than in the countryside, where life is usually slower. Cities have a lot to offer both **residents** who live there, and also visitors in terms of culture, with cinemas, theatres, shops and restaurants. However there may also be drawbacks to city life. Cities can be noisy, crowded and congested, and can suffer from pollution.

DETECTIVE WORK
How many people live in your nearest city? Use the Internet to find out by typing the name of the city and 'population' into a search engine. Or investigate at your local library.

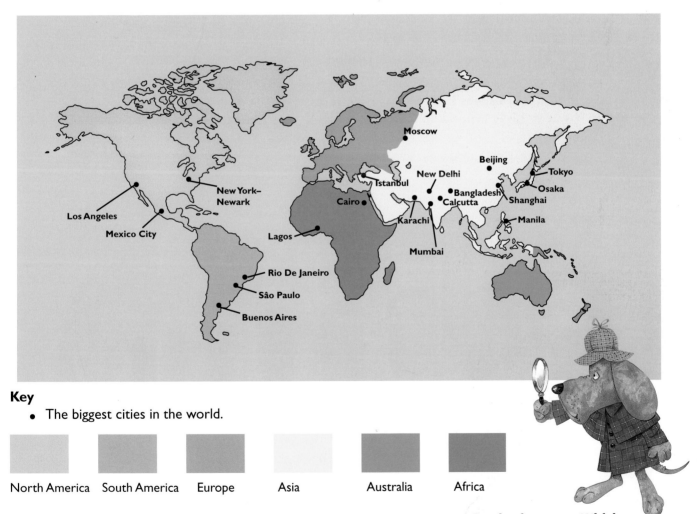

Key
- The biggest cities in the world.

North America | South America | Europe | Asia | Australia | Africa

This map shows the world's 20 biggest cities. Some are in developed countries such as the United States, but many lie in developing countries and regions such as South America and Africa.

Study the map. Which continent contains the highest number of the biggest cities?

How do cities form?

Many cities are old, and some were **founded** thousands of years ago. The very first cities grew up around 6,000 years ago in the Middle East. Somewhat later, cities appeared in India and Pakistan, Egypt and China.

All settlements form in places where food and water, vital to life, are available. Many cities have grown up along rivers that provided water and fertile land for farming. Later the rivers were used for trade and transport. Towns also grew up along the coast, where the sea provided food and transport. Ports on natural harbours, such as Venice (Italy), Istanbul (Turkey) and New York (United States), became centres for trade.

The Colosseum in Rome, Italy was built to stage contests and spectacles. It was finished around 80 CE.

FOCUS ON

Ancient Rome

The city of Rome was founded in the 8th century BCE. By 100 CE Rome had become the centre of a mighty **empire** covering much of Europe, the Middle East and the North African coast. At this time Rome held over a million people. Roman architects built fine public buildings and aqueducts to bring water to the city. Paved roads stretched from Rome to the far corners of the empire.

Many cities grew as major ports on rivers where ocean-going ships could dock. This is Paris on the River Seine.

Defence was important to city people in ancient times. Settlements grew up in places that could be defended against enemies, such as on hills that provided lookout points, or rivers that formed a barrier to invasion. Many cities were fortified with high walls that provided safety in times of war.

Cities also grew up in areas that offered useful resources such as timber and minerals. Some cities owe their **origins** entirely to mineral wealth. For example, the town of Kimberley in Australia was founded at a remote site where diamonds were discovered in the 1870s. Kimberley is now a city whose wealth is based on the diamond trade. Johannesburg in South Africa grew up at a site where gold was found in the 1880s.

Study the photo of Paris. What are the advantages of the position? Can you see any disadvantages?

DETECTIVE WORK

How old is your city or town? Find out using the Internet or your local library. Study the city's location on a local map. What are the advantages of the site?

How do cities expand and develop?

Until a few hundred years ago, relatively few people lived in cities. In 1800, just 2.5 per cent of the world's population lived in urban areas. By 1980 that figure had risen to 40 per cent. In 2010 it is expected to reach 55 per cent.

FOCUS ON

Glasgow

From the late 1700s, Glasgow grew rapidly following **industrialisation**. Located on the River Clyde close to rich coalfields, Glasgow became a major centre for ship-building and heavy industry. From a town of 84,000 people in 1800, it grew to contain half a million people by 1870. Glasgow's industries later declined, but it remains the fourth largest city in the UK.

From the late 1700s, advances in technology led to the **Industrial Revolution** in Europe and North America. Cities such as Glasgow in Scotland and Chicago, United States, grew quickly as centres of manufacturing. People moved from country areas to work in factories, and lived in nearby housing, often in poverty. In the 1900s, developing regions in parts of Africa, Asia and South America industrialised rapidly, and their cities grew quickly as a result.

In the 1950s, factory workers in Glasgow lived in poor conditions. In this slum area, called the Gorbals, conditions were polluted and overcrowded.

In 1870 Mumbai's population was just 640,000. It is now home to over 18 million people – one of the very largest cities in the world.

During the 1900s, the world's population increased rapidly, thanks to improvements in health and food production. In 1900 the world's population was just 1.6 billion. By 1950 it had risen to 2.5 billion, and to 5.2 billion by 1990. By 2012 it is expected to reach 7 billion. City populations expand as local people start families, and also as people move in from the countryside to find work.

As cities expand, they draw increasingly on the resources of the surrounding area, such as food, timber and minerals. With the growth of international trade, cities are now supplied with resources from all over the world. If a city grows very quickly, it can put a strain on local resources and the environment.

Cities with more than 10 million people are known as megacities. These can form when neighbouring cities spread across the countryside to merge with one another. In eastern United States, the cities of New York, Boston and Washington now form one huge urban area. Elsewhere, a single city, such as Mumbai in India, has grown quickly to form a **megacity**.

DETECTIVE WORK
Use the Internet or local library to find out the population of your city or town 50 years ago and 100 years ago. Find out about major changes that have happened in the city in the last 50 or 100 years.

How are cities organised?

Cities are laid out in different ways, but all contain zones with different functions. For example, there are **residential** areas where people live, industrial zones with many factories, and commercial districts where offices are based.

This aerial view shows the centre of Sydney. On the left you can see the Sydney Opera House.

In cities such as London, these zones are arranged in rings around a central business district. This is the main commercial area with banks, shops and offices. Surrounding this is often an old industrial zone, which may have been rebuilt, and now has new flats and offices. Further out are the inner and outer **suburbs**, where most people live.

The oldest part of the city often lies in the centre, with newer districts appearing on the outskirts as the city expands. Not all cities are laid out like this. Los Angeles (United States) and Tokyo (Japan) developed from several centres, which later merged.

Many cities contain an area known as the CBD. What do you think these initials stand for?

FOCUS ON

Maps called land use maps show the different zones within a city. For example, residential, industrial and commercial zones and open spaces are shown in different colours. These maps help council workers and are also used by planners.

In many cities, the central business district is becoming less defined as companies move to the suburbs. Some suburbs have grown so huge they are now cities in their own right. There are many of these so-called **'boomburgs'** in the United States.

All cities have an **infrastructure**, made up of all the **services** that are needed to keep the city running smoothly. The infrastructure includes schools and hospitals. It also includes police and fire services, transport systems, and even the provision of water, electricity and sewerage. The city council is responsible for maintaining many of these services, and the better they are managed, the higher the standard of living is likely to be.

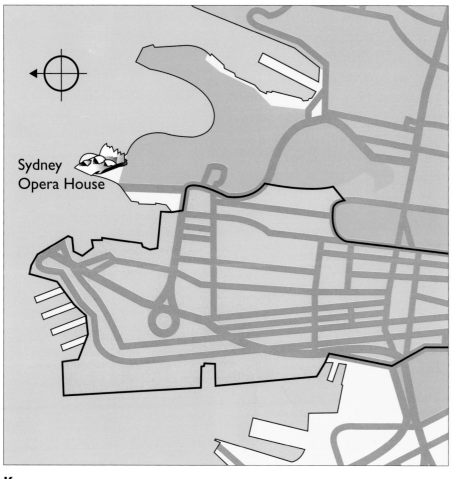

This landuse map shows the same area of Sydney as the photo opposite.

Key

Central Business District   Parks   Residential   Other

DETECTIVE WORK

Try to find a land use map showing your nearest city or your local neighbourhood. Try the city council website or ask at your local library. Compare it to a local street map.

What work do people do in cities?

Work is the main thing that attracts people to cities. There are far more jobs and a greater variety of work in cities than there is in smaller settlements. Cities themselves expand when there is plenty of work to attract people from the local area, but the population can also shrink if work becomes scarce.

All the different jobs people do in cities can be divided into just a few main areas called **sectors**. Some people work in factories, processing raw materials, such as metal or wood to make goods such as furniture. This is the manufacturing sector. Other workers run all the services needed to keep the city going, from transport, schools, hospitals, shops and local government to emergency services. This is the service sector. This sector also includes business or banking. In addition, other people work at home, keeping house and raising a family.

FOCUS ON

Capital cities

Capital cities have a special function as home to the nation's government. Some capitals have grown up near the centre of the country. However some countries choose to build new capitals, sometimes in remote places with a particular advantage, such as lots of space or a favourable climate. Islamabad, the capital of Pakistan, lies in the north where the climate is more comfortable than elsewhere.

In the 1960s the capital of Brazil was relocated from Rio de Janeiro on the coast to the new city of Brasilia in the central highlands.

Not everyone in a city can find work. People who can't are unemployed. **Unemployment** is likely to be high in cities that are expanding rapidly. Hundreds and even thousands of people move to these cities each week in search of work, but there are not enough jobs to go round. Some of the new arrivals get by doing casual work, for example on a building site or selling goods on the street.

What are buildings like in cities?

Cities contain many different types of buildings. As well as grand public buildings and monuments, there may be high-rise office blocks, housing of various kinds, shopping centres, factories and power stations. A single building style dominates a few cities, but most have buildings from many different periods, in all sorts of styles.

Space is particularly cramped in cities built on islands. Manhattan Island in the centre of New York has many high-rise buildings.

A large number of people in any city live in the suburbs, whether in housing estates, apartment blocks or other accommodation. In older cities, suburban areas developed when railways and other transport networks were built. This allowed people to live outside the centre and travel in to work. This is called commuting. Out in the suburbs, there is usually more room to build than in the cramped inner city, so houses can be laid out with gardens, providing better living conditions.

DETECTIVE WORK

Investigate the housing in your neighbourhood. Make a list of all the types of housing you see, such as blocks of flats, bungalows, **detached** and terraced houses. You could draw or photograph the different building styles you see. Do you live near the city centre or in a suburb?

Lack of space is often a problem in the centre, especially where the site is hemmed in by the sea, a river or mountains. If the city cannot expand outward, the only way to build is upwards. High-rise buildings dominate the centre or **downtown areas** of most cities, including London, Paris, New York, Tokyo in Japan, and Shanghai in China.

Many cities around the world contain **slums** – districts with poor-quality housing which are often very crowded. Basic services such as running water, electricity and sewerage are often inadequate, and schools, medical centres and other services are scarce. In many slums, rubbish is not collected, but builds up on the streets. Cities in developing parts of the world may have slums, but poor housing also exists in more developed regions such as Europe and North America.

This boy lives in the South Bronx in New York. Around him is poor slum housing.

Shanty towns

Fast-growing cities often contain **shanty towns**, where homes are built of makeshift materials such as corrugated iron and even cardboard. Shanty towns spring up when many people move to the city to seek work, but have nowhere to live. They end up building temporary shelters using whatever materials they can find.

How do people enjoy themselves in cities?

Cities offer a huge range of leisure activities to help people enjoy their free time. Every city has its cafés, restaurants, shopping centres and markets. There are sports centres, stadiums, and also parks and other open spaces, where people can relax or enjoy their favourite sport.

Cities are centres of culture and entertainment. People go to cinemas, theatres, art galleries and museums. In some cities, theatres and cinemas are concentrated in one area, such as Broadway in New York, or London's West End. Cities also have places of worship for people of different faiths, such as churches, synagogues and mosques. People from different backgrounds enrich the city's culture in many ways, perhaps not least in the range of foods and styles of cooking in shops and restaurants.

DETECTIVE WORK

Make a list of all the leisure facilities you can think of in your town or city. Ask your friends and family to list their top three leisure activities. You could make a chart to show the results.

Some tourist attractions are old buildings. Others, such as the London Eye, are newly built.

Green spaces are important for leisure and also the well-being of city people. Sports such as cricket are played in Mumbai and in city parks all over the world.

In many cities, special events such as festivals take place at particular times of year. People take to the streets for parades with music, singing and dancing. For example, the Catholic festival of Mardi Gras (Shrove Tuesday), which falls before Easter, is marked by carnivals in many cities in Europe and the Americas, including New Orleans in southern United States and Rio de Janeiro in Brazil.

A city's culture and leisure activities are enjoyed by residents and visitors. Tourism is important in many cities. It is central to the economy of a few cities, such as the Spanish seaside **resort** of Benidorm, the historic city of Venice in Italy, and Las Vegas, United States, a centre of gambling and entertainment.

FOCUS ON

Las Vegas

Las Vegas in western United States has an economy based on leisure and entertainment. It grew up as a centre for gambling and has a main street lined with spectacular casinos. Las Vegas is located in the Nevada Desert. The tourist industry brings in great wealth but also drains local resources, particularly water, which affects people such as farmers.

How do people get about in cities?

A good transport network is essential to the smooth running of any city. Cities grow up around the focus of local transport routes, for example a crossing point on a river, or at the foot of a pass through the mountains. As the city grows, its transport network develops to link it to other settlements in the region.

In most parts of the world, cities are now connected by a network of fast roads and rail routes. If you look at a map of almost any city you will see it lies at the heart of a transport network, with routes spreading out in all directions. People may travel to and from the city by car, coach, train, boat – or by plane, since many cities have national or international airports.

DETECTIVE WORK
List all the forms of transport people use in your town or city. What are the advantages of each form? Can you think of any disadvantages?

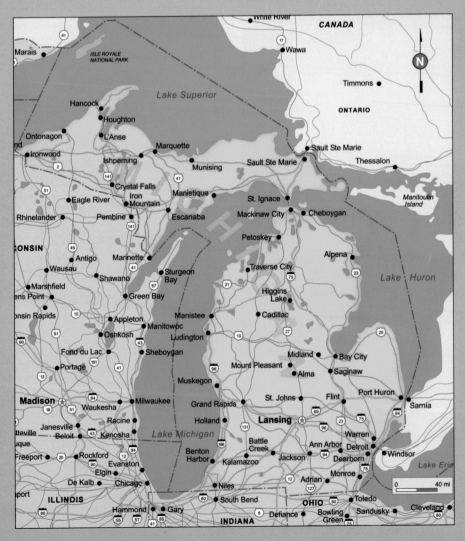

This map shows the major transport network around Lake Michigan in the United States. Railroads are marked in green, highways (motorways) in orange and airports are shown with stars.

Study the map.
List all the forms of transport you might use to get from Lansing, Michigan to Madison, Wisconsin.

In cities such as Taipei in Taiwan, Southeast Asia, many people used to get to work by bicycle or motorbike. Car use has grown quickly in recent years.

Once inside the city, people may get around on foot, and by car, bus, train or tram. Some people ride bicycles or motorbikes, while others hire taxis or local forms of transport, such as **cycle-rickshaws.** Many major cities have an underground railway network that carries huge numbers of people during rush hours, when people travel to and from work. On Tokyo's underground, officials called pushers are employed to squeeze as many **commuters** as possible into each carriage.

Traffic is a major problem in a great many cities. Despite many forms of public transport, people still choose to drive into the city centre, and car use is rising rapidly in many cities in developing countries. Narrow streets are clogged with vehicles during rush hours. As well as congestion, road traffic causes noise and pollution. Space for parking is very limited in many city centres.

FOCUS ON

One way to tackle city **congestion** is to charge motorists and truck drivers a fee for entering the centre. In 2003 a **congestion charge** was introduced in London. It led to a 15 per cent reduction in traffic. The funds raised by the charge are used to improve public transport, which further relieves congestion.

Why are some cities under threat?

Around the world, many cities have grown up in areas that are at risk from natural disasters, such as earthquakes or volcanic eruptions. Flooding is a major risk in some cities. As well as natural disasters, there are other kinds of threats, such as war and disease.

In 2008 an earthquake wrecked the city of Yingxiu in China.

A number of cities around the world are located close to volcanoes. People settle in volcanic regions because the soil is fertile, and in some places, there are valuable minerals such as gold or diamonds. The modern city of Naples, in southern Italy, lies in the shadow of Mount Vesuvius, which destroyed the Roman city of Pompeii in 79 CE. One day the volcano might erupt again. Many cities lie in zones prone to earthquakes. In 1995, the Japanese city of Kobe was devastated by an earthquake. Fire broke out and 5,000 people died.

FOCUS ON

Tsunamis

Floods can strike coastal cities because of tsunamis – tidal waves, which are usually triggered by earthquakes. In December 2004, coastal cities in Indonesia and Thailand were devastated by tsunamis following an undersea earthquake in the Indian Ocean. Over 100,000 people died in Banda Aceh, Indonesia, the district nearest the quake.

DETECTIVE WORK

Find out more about cities at risk of natural hazards using your local library or the Internet. Type key words such as 'cities at risk' and the name of the hazard, such as earthquake or tsunami, into a search engine.

Flooding is a danger in many coastal and low-lying cities. Flooding may occur if the local river bursts its banks after very heavy rain, or if a hurricane blows in from the ocean, bringing a surge of water called a **storm surge**. In 2005, the city of New Orleans in southern USA was devastated by flooding in the wake of a hurricane.

Natural disasters are not the only threats to cities worldwide. In times of war, cities are at risk of enemy attack. There may also be a risk of terrorism. In 2001, the World Trade Center in New York was wrecked by a terrorist attack. In 2008, the city of Mumbai, India, was targeted by terrorists. Disease is another danger. Diseases such as **cholera** can spread rapidly in cities where there is overcrowding and poor sanitation, and where clean water is scarce.

In 2005, New Orleans was hit by severe flooding in the wake of Hurricane Katrina, after a storm surge breached local flood defences.

Many cities around the world have grown up on estuaries, where rivers enter the ocean. Why could these cities be at risk?

What are the problems in cities?

Most cities offer a huge range of opportunities in terms of work, culture and leisure activities. They are often dynamic and exciting places to live. However, cities everywhere also suffer from problems such as congestion, poverty and pollution.

Experts estimate that up to one-third of all people in cities are living in poverty. The number of poor people is likely to be high in developing parts of the world, but in every city there is poverty. Poverty is linked to unemployment. People who cannot find a job or who work for very low wages struggle to provide food and other essentials for their families. Often, it is the poorest families who live in slums or run-down areas, where services are inadequate.

A form of pollution called smog is often worst in cities located in low-lying areas between hills or mountains. This is true of many cities such as Mexico City.

In every city, some people are well-off and enjoy a high standard of living. Where there is inequality and a gulf develops between rich and poor, it can cause tensions between different parts of the **community**. If this happens, crime and violence can rise.

DETECTIVE WORK
Carry out a litter survey in your neighbourhood. Do you see litter on the streets? Are there places where rubbish bins are overflowing? Identify the sorts of litter that have been dropped, for example, bottles, tins, paper, or plastic packaging.

Pollution is a problem in most urban areas. Vehicles, factories, power stations and homes release waste gases as they burn **fossil fuels** such as oil and coal for energy. The waste gases can produce a dirty haze called **smog**, which hangs over many cities. Air pollution causes breathing problems such as asthma. In some cities people who work outdoors wear masks to avoid breathing in polluted air. Pollution is likely to be a serious hazard in countries that are industrialising rapidly, such as India and China.

Waste disposal is a major challenge for city authorities. Every day, people produce vast amounts of waste, which has to be disposed of somehow. Rubbish may be trucked outside the city and either buried in pits called **landfill sites**, or burned in **incinerators**, but both of these methods cause pollution. Rubbish that is not collected regularly builds up on the streets or in drains and threatens people's health.

In developing countries, city authorities may not have the funds to deal with the vast amounts of waste created daily. These poor people in Manila in the Philippines, Southeast Asia, are sifting through mountains of trash in search of things that are useful or can be sold.

How can cities be improved?

City authorities face a difficult task. It is their responsibility to maintain all the city's services. The money for this comes from taxes paid by workers, and in some cases from central government or charities. However, many cities struggle to pay for all the services people need.

In cities such as **San Francisco** in the **United States, electric trams provide an efficient transport service that causes less pollution.**

Improving people's lives and tackling poverty are top **priorities** for many city **councils**. If poverty can be reduced it reduces the gap between rich and poor, and so eases social tensions. The crime rate is likely to fall.

The key to tackling poverty is often to create more jobs and provide better training and education. One way forward is to increase public spending on housing.

DETECTIVE WORK

Ask your family and friends how they think your neighbourhood could best be improved. Ask them to list their three top priorities among these measures: improving public transport; increasing open spaces; reducing traffic; improving shops and leisure facilities; providing better housing; making the city clean and safe. Make a chart to show the results.

Building better housing improves people's lives and also creates jobs. However the city may lack the funds to spend more without raising taxes, which will be unpopular with tax-payers.

Many city authorities tackle pollution by passing laws that require factories and power stations to reduce or clean up the waste gases they produce. Industries that cause a lot of pollution can be fined. Air pollution can also be tackled by reducing the amount of traffic. This can be done in many ways, for example by making the centre traffic-free. Many councils have introduced park-and-ride schemes which encourage motorists to leave their cars in the suburbs and take a bus to the centre. But often, people will only leave their cars at home if public transport is improved enough to make their journey easier.

FOCUS ON

Reduce, reuse, recycle

In cities across the world, councils are tackling the problem of waste disposal by encouraging people to reduce, reuse and recycle. Every family can reduce the amount of waste it produces by buying goods with less packaging, and reusing items such as plastic bags. Bottles, tins, paper and plastic can be returned to **recycling** centres so the materials can be used again.

Why does improving public transport help to reduce congestion on city streets?

Encouraging recycling helps to tackle the problem of waste disposal.

What will cities be like in the future?

Cities in many parts of the world have grown a lot in recent years. In future, urban areas will continue to expand. This will create a need for more housing, more jobs, better transport, more leisure activities and other services – a major challenge for the authorities involved.

When cities expand, new housing estates and shopping centres spread over what was once countryside. This is Silicon Valley in the United States.

By 2050, experts estimate that two-thirds of the world's population will live in urban areas. The cities that are likely to expand the fastest are mostly in developing countries – the very areas where councils often lack the money to improve services. In more developed countries, some cities may actually shrink, as people move out of the suburbs to the countryside beyond, where conditions are less noisy and congested. Advances in technology such as the Internet allow people to work from home rather than commuting. Businesses also relocate to rural areas. All of this may cause city populations to shrink, but it can also increase urban development in the countryside.

DETECTIVE WORK

Investigate plans for new developments in your town or city. You could try logging onto the council website or visit the local planning department. How do you think your city should develop in the future? You could email your ideas to the council.

27

As cities and other urban areas grow, they put increasing pressure on wild countryside. Open areas inside cities also get swallowed up by new developments, so that there are fewer parks and green spaces. City planners can tackle this problem by redeveloping waste ground, such as disused factories and warehouses. These areas are known as **brownfield sites.** In some countries, governments pass laws to restrict development in the countryside around cities. These areas are known as **green belts.**

FOCUS ON

Sustainability

Many councils nowadays are working to make cities more **sustainable.** This means using all kinds of resources carefully, so that there will be enough resources for the future. Councils aim to improve conditions for citizens while harming the environment as little as possible. For example, when new housing estates are built, houses can be designed to use non-polluting forms of energy, such as solar power. Improving public transport, reducing pollution and providing green spaces will all help to make cities more sustainable – and nicer places in which to live!

Sustainable cities need green spaces. In Singapore in Southeast Asia, waste ground has been converted into new parks.

Your project

I f you've done the detective work throughout the book and answered all of Sherlock's questions, you now know a lot about cities! You could produce your own project about cities using this information.

First you'll need to choose a subject that interests you. You could take one of these questions as a starting point.

Topic questions
- Find out all you can about your town or city. When was the city founded, and why and when did it expand most quickly? What are the main types of work that go on? How has the settlement changed over the years? What problems are there, and how are they being tackled? What plans are there to improve the city?
- Compare life in a city in a developed region, for example in western Europe or North America, with one in a developing part of the world, for example in Africa, Asia or South America. What are the main similarities and differences between the two cities? Which city would you prefer to live in?
- Find out more about the world's very largest cities, by typing the word 'megacity' into a search engine. Why are these cities growing so fast?

Sherlock has done a project about the animals that live wild in cities. He has found out that foxes, raccoons, mice, squirrels and birds such as pigeons and sparrows all thrive in busy cities around the world.

Architects design new buildings for cities.

Your local library and the Internet can provide all sorts of information. You could present your project in an interesting way, perhaps using one of the ideas below.

Hong Kong has many skyscrapers.

Project presentation
- Make a map of your city and its surroundings in the centre of a large piece of paper. Stick photos, sketches and charts around the edge showing important sites and city life.
- Imagine you are making a TV documentary about life in the city. Decide what themes you want to bring out, what activities you want to film, and a list of people, such as council officials and architects to interview.
- Imagine you are writing a tourist brochure about life in the city. Plan a structure to include a short history of the city and the main attractions. You might include a description of public transport and important leisure facilities.

Cars aren't allowed in this street in Seoul, South Korea.

Glossary

boomburg City that has grown from a suburb.

brownfield site An area that has been built on before.

city A settlement with over 50,000 people.

cholera A disease caused by drinking polluted water.

community A settlement or district, also the people who live there.

commuter Someone who travels to and from work.

congestion Overcrowding on the streets, usually caused by traffic or people.

congestion charge A charge paid by the drivers of private vehicles entering some cities.

council An organisation that governs a settlement and provides services.

cycle-rickshaws Three-wheeled vehicles powered by cyclists.

detached Separate.

developed country A country where the industries and economy are well developed.

developing country A country where the industries and economy are not fully developed.

downtown area City centre.

empire A group of areas or nations ruled over by a single power.

ethnic To do with race.

fossil fuels Fuels such as coal, oil and gas, which are made from the fossilized remains of plants or animals.

found [a settlement] When the first buildings in a settlement were constructed.

green belt An area around a city where building is carefully controlled.

immigrant A person who arrives from another country to live.

incinerator Hot furnace in which rubbish is burned.

industrialisation When a country develops its industries.

Industrial Revolution The period in the late 1700s and 1800s which saw many advances in technology and the growth of factories.

infrastructure All the services and facilities needed for a city or town to run smoothly.

landfill site A pit where rubbish is buried.

megacity A city with more than 10 million people.

origin Beginning.

population All the people who live in a particular place, such as a country, city or smaller settlement.

priority Something which is considered important.

recycling When waste materials such as glass, plastic and paper are used to make new materials.

resident A person who lives in a settlement.

residential Of an urban area where many people live.

resort A village, town or city which people visit for leisure or health reasons.

rural Of or belonging to the countryside.

sector Part of something.

settlement Place where people live, such as a village, town or city.

services The systems in a city or smaller settlement that supply public needs, from schools and hospitals to police and fire services, and also the supply of gas, electricity and water.

shanty town Settlement that has been built using makeshift materials such as scraps of wood and metal.

slum An area with poor-quality, run-down housing.

smog A poisonous haze caused by air pollution.

storm surge Surging water produced by a hurricane.

suburb Outlying area of a city where many people live.

sustainable To manage resources so that they will not run out in future, and so as to cause little harm to the environment.

unemployment When people cannot find work.

urban Of or belonging to a town or city.

Answers

page 5: Asia is the continent with the largest number of huge cities.

page 7: The location of Paris on the River Seine provided fresh water and fertile land for farming. The river was also useful for defence and transport, but there is a risk of flooding after heavy rain.

page 10: CBD is short for Central Business District.

page 13: A bus driver and anyone involved in helping to run a city's public transport network works in the service sector.

page 18: The map shows you can travel between Lansing and Madison by road or rail, or take a plane!

page 21: Cities on estuaries may be at risk of flooding either when the river swells after heavy rain or, in some parts of the world, after a storm surge hits during a hurricane.

page 25: The more people that use public transport, the less private cars there will be on roads. It is private vehicles that cause most of the congestion in cities.

Further Information

Further reading
Cities, Towns and Villages by Jen Green
(Franklin Watts, 2007)

The Growth of Cities by Robert Snedden
(Franklin Watts, 2003)

Looking at Settlements by Judith Anderson
(Franklin Watts, 2006)

Websites
Websites about settlements

Globaleye
Website has information about cities around the world.
www.globaleye.org.uk/secondary

World City Photos
A selection of photographs of cities around the world.
www.worldcityphotos.org

Websites about cities and the environment:

Development Education
A site on sustainable cities.
www.dep.org.uk/scities/index.php

Sustainable cities
www.sustainable-cities.org.uk/

Environment Agency
www.environment-agency.gov.uk

Index

The Geography Detective Investigates

Contents of titles in the series:

WAYLAND